Self-portrait with palette (detail), 1891 Oil on canvas, 55 x 46 cm - USA, Private collection

GAUGUIN

"What sort of a man is he then? He is Gauguin, the savage who hates the restrictions of society. He has something of the Titan, that rebel who, jealous of the Creator, makes his own little creature in his spare time; the child who dismantles its toys in order to make new ones."

August Strindberg

Even by the bohemian standards of other contemporary artists, there was something extremely forceful, even wild, about Gauguin - both as a man and as an artist. His paintings, daring in colour, form and content, seemed to unveil a menacing, as well as a primitive, side to nature. His life, instead of settling down to a reasonably tranquil old age, seemed reversed; he abandoned his family and lucrative job to wander round the globe, dying ill, impoverished and alone on an obscure Pacific island. Yet considering his background and upbringing, such a restless wandering pattern in his life looks less surprising; for his art such wandering was essential.

His father, Clovis Gauguin, was a radical political journalist, and his mother was a fiery feminist of aristocratic Peruvian descent. Paul Gauguin was born in Paris on 7 June 1848. He was only two when his father took the family off to Peru, fleeing political repression. His father died on the voyage out but the family's stay of five years there had a crucial impact on the young Gauguin, who never forgot the exotic lure of the tropics. He was seven when he returned to school in Orléans, a city he found suffocatingly provincial. To escape it he became a sailor at the age of 16 and did his military service in the navy, which he left in 1871.

His guardian, Gustave Arosa, an admirer and collector of the Impressionist Pissarro, arranged for him to be taken on by the stockbroker Bertin. The young Gauguin had a flair for business. In 1873, he married a Danish girl, Mette Sophie Gad. At this point, Paul Gauguin's future must have seemed securely mapped out; he had five children, a large house and made plenty of money, some of which he spent on collecting paintings by modern artists. In his free time he painted with his colleague, Emile Schuffenecker. From 1880 onwards, he took part in the Impressionists' exhibitions, after being introduced by Pissarro, to whom he was both patron and pupil. Among Gauguin's exhibited pieces were marble busts showing a concern for form that would set him apart from the Impressionists' obsession with light.

But beneath this apparently respectable exterior, Gauguin, with his mixed aristocratic and vagabond background, must have felt intolerable pressures building up. They exploded in 1883 when he was 35. Gauguin now decided that he must choose between his money-making work (not going so well since a banking crisis in 1882) and his painting. He no longer hesitated: at the beginning of 1883, he left his job with Bertin, without even telling his wife of his decision, filled with an almost fanatical desire to paint. Although he tried hard to support his family at first - selling his collection of modern paintings and trying to get commissions for his own work - he failed. His wife took the children to her home in Copenhagen, and soon his links with his family became tenuous as his art came to possess him.

In 1886, he began visiting Brittany, attracted by its densely wooded, haunting landscapes, its still powerful peasant traditions and its general distance from what he increasingly saw as a corrupt "civilisation". It was in the fishing village of Pont-Aven that he first met the young painter, Emile Bernard, whose radical style paralleled and influenced his own.

Caricature self-portrait of Gauguin, painted on the panel of a wardrobe in the inn of Marie Henry at Le Pouldu, 1889 - Oil on wood, 80 x 52 cm - Washington D.C., National Gallery of Art, Chester Day Collection.

In a further flight from civilisation, he set out with Laval, another painter, for Panama in April 1887. There Gauguin worked briefly as a labourer on the Panama canal, before going on to Martinique. From there Gauguin returned home in November. This renewed contact with the tropics had stimulated and transformed his art, as is shown by the vividness of *St. Peter's Bay* (page 4).

Gauguin's friend and former colleague Schuffenecker helped him on his return to Paris, when he met the Dutch brothers Vincent and Theo Van Gogh. These two admired his work enormously. Theo organized an exhibition in his gallery in 1888, but Gauguin's canvases failed to sell. Gauguin himself returned to Brittany, where he painted and made sculptures and pottery, amid a group of painters, including Emile Bernard and Laval. It was now that he painted his first truly original masterpiece - *The Vision After The Sermon* (page 8) - breaking completely from the

Group of painters in front of the Pension Gloanec in Pont-Aven, in a photograph from 1888. Gauguin is seated third from the right in the front row sitting on the kerb.

Gauguin painting in Schuffenecker's garden - Photograph, c. 1889.

Impressionist style, using areas of pure colour in an unrealistic way.

He joined Van Gogh, with whom he had been exchanging letters about art, in Arles in October, painting *Les Alyscamps* (page 6). The two men did not get on, however; Gauguin admired the great classicists like Raphael, Ingres and Degas whom Van Gogh hated. Further, Gauguin found the Dutchman increasingly unstable mentally. Finally Van Gogh threatened Gauguin with a razor; Gauguin fled the house.

Gauguin then returned to Brittany. The Café Volpini exhibition during the International Exhibition in 1889 was another failure, but his work had now aroused the interest of young painters and critics. At the end of 1890, he attended the meetings of the Symbolists in the Café Voltaire in Paris. The Symbolists were trying to escape from what they saw as the dreary realism of the Impressionists and express instead the mystical and occult; Gauguin's emerging style, with its increasingly literary or mystical side, appealed to Symbolist writers like Albert Aurier and

the poet Stephan Mallarmé, who became his friends. Mallarmé presided over a banquet given in his honour in 1891. Despite his recognition by this group, Gauguin had already decided to leave France and search for an unspoilt paradise in the Pacific.

In the book *Noa Noa* he wrote about his life in Tahiti: "I have escaped from everything artificial... Here I enter into truth... After the disease of civilisation, life in this new world is a return to health." In fact, his first stay in Tahiti was not a total success, for the island was a French colony, not an untouched paradise of gracious natives and sexual freedom, yet he found he could no longer live without its climate and freedom. Besides, in Paris, where he returned in August 1893, one disappointment followed another; an exhibition flopped, an auction was a disaster, a final visit to his wife in Copenhagen came to nothing. With some inherited money he went back to Tahiti in 1895, never to return to France.

Alone, suffering from many ailments as well as syphilis (always a passionate man, Gauguin had married a thirteen year old Tahitian girl bigamously as well as having had many mistresses both

Drawing from Old Maori Cults, *c. 1892.*

Sketch for the self-portrait called Les Misérables, *in a letter of 8 October to Schuffenecker Private Collection.*

in France and Tahiti) he painted his greatest canvas *Where Do We Come From? What Are We? Where Are We Going To?* (page 20). Then, seemingly emptied of all desire, he attempted suicide in 1898 by swallowing arsenic. Amazingly, he survived and set to work once again.

In this final period Gauguin painted some of his most evocative scenes of paradise regained in the Pacific, such as *Tahitian Girls With Flowers* (page 26), but his life was not in reality idyllic. He had no time for the extremely petty conventions of colonials; officialdom in turn distrusted this wild bohemian who had "gone native". He left Tahiti in 1901 to seek refuge on the small island of Dominica.

Life was not much easier there and his health deteriorated. The colonial officials saw him as a threat and in May 1903 he was condemned to jail. Shattered by these pressures, Paul Gauguin died on 8 May 1903. Within three years an exhibition in Paris attracted hordes of painters and buyers; he is now considered one of the greatest influences on modern art.

SAINT PETER'S BAY

1887 - Oil on canvas , 54.5 x 89.8 cm
Copenhagen, Ny Carlsberg Glpotek

Early in April 1887, Gauguin wrote to his wife, whom he was still trying to impress: "My reputation as an artist is growing daily, but in the meantime I sometimes go for as long as three days without food, which not only ruins my health but also saps my energy. I must regain the latter and I am going to Panama to live "wild". I know a little island in the Pacific. I shall take my paints and brushes and immerse myself in life far away from anybody".
After a first period in Panama, where Gauguin worked on the Panama Canal, he arrived in Martinique. Here he painted this idyllic portrayal of *St. Peter's Bay*. Gauguin was completely overwhelmed by the lush, wild vegetation and the vibrant glowing colours of the tropics, of which he still retained vivid childhood memories, and he was inspired to recreate their magnificence in his paintings. He did so with a naturalness lacking in most of his later tropical pictures. This produced a painting which is immediately appealing in its fresh bright colours and idyllic setting.

Huts Under The Trees, *1887 - Oil on canvas, 92 cm x 72 cm - USA, private collection.*

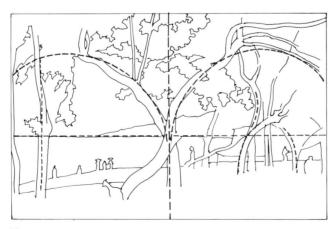

The composition of the picture is based on the two trees in the centre foreground. They cross over, forming an arch almost like stage curtains beyond which is the dazzling panorama across the bay.

USE OF COLOUR
The tones are emphasised by the contrast between them: the blue of the sea (1), the green of the trees (2) and the warm tones of the sandy earth (3).

1   2   3

LES ALYSCAMPS

1888 - Oil on canvas, 92 x 73 cm
Paris, Musée d'Orsay

In a letter Gauguin wrote to his friend Emile Bernard, he said: "I am at Arles. Both the countryside and the people seem so provincial that I feel quite out of place. Vincent and I disagree violently on most things, particularly painting. He admires Daumier and Theodore Rousseau, all painters that I can't stand; and he loathes painters I admire: Ingres, Raphael and Degas. I say "Captain, you are right" just to keep the peace."

Van Gogh wrote to his brother Theo: "Gauguin and I talk a lot about Delacroix, Rembrandt, etc. Our discussions are highly charged - sometimes we emerge, our minds like spent batteries...".

In October 1888, Gauguin had arrived at Arles where Van Gogh, whom he had known for some time, was awaiting him. Despite their mutual respect and admiration, they clashed continuously over many things, including painting. Gauguin was obsessed with a desire to translate what he saw into synthetic and symbolic form. Synthetism, by which he meant that form and colour should be simplified but intensified for the sake of expressiveness, was by now the keynote of his work. "Don't imitate nature too closely," he said. "Art is an abstraction; draw on nature for inspiration but think more about the creative process than the result".

The countryside, the light and the colours of Arles fascinated the Dutchman but left Gauguin relatively unmoved - perhaps it was too flat after Britanny. But he found the inhabitants of Arles enchanting subjects, elegant and passionate, recalling to him images of the ancient Romans. In *Les Alyscamps* (an ancient cemetery dating back to pre-Christian days), the dominant colours are various shades of green, which contrast with the orange backdrop of trees. While still remaining half within the confines of tradition, the 1888 works are carefully thought out. They have simple, balanced compositions. Sometimes they are decorative, sometimes mystical: the essence of Synthetism.

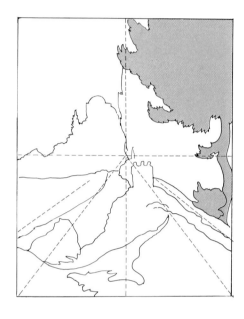

COMPOSITION
Conventionally based upon the central convergence of lines of perspective, the composition is softened by the curves of the paths through the greenery and by the form of the trees.

The cemetery at Alyscamps inspired many works by both Gauguin and Van Gogh, although it is difficult to pinpoint any mutual influence. Van Gogh's version Les Alyscamps, Dead Leaves - Canvas, 1888 - Otterlo, Rijksmuseum Kroller-Muller - plays on the contrast between the blues of the trunks of the avenue of trees in the foreground and the orange carpet of dead leaves standing out against the green meadows in the background.

THE VISION AFTER THE SERMON

1888 - Oil on canvas, 73 x 92 cm
Edinburgh, The National Gallery of Scotland.

In 1888 at Pont-Aven, Gauguin was re-acquainted with the young Emile Bernard, whom he had first encountered two years earlier. This meeting proved to be profoundly influential on Gauguin's work. Bernard was both painter and thinker, with a mystical bent. His way of spreading blocks of colour in simple shapes, and defining them in the style of stained glass windows or Limoges enamel, gave birth to a style known as "cloisonnism". The term is drawn from cloisonné enamel. For Gauguin, it provided an opportunity to move away from Impressionist naturalism, which he felt was still constricting him. *The Vision After The Sermon* (also known as *Jacob And The Angel)* clearly demonstrates Gauguin's commitment to Bernard's theory of cloisonnism, both in form and concept. This influence was so strong that Bernard claimed: "In *The Vision After The Sermon*, he not only applied the colour theory which I had discussed with him, but he also adopted the particular style of my *Breton Women In The Green Meadow*. He put the same large figures in huge châtelaine bonnets in the foreground." Gauguin may have been influenced by his friend's work, but he was convinced that he had said something new in his picture. He explained in a letter to Van Gogh dated September 1888: "I believe that in these figures, I have achieved a great sense of rustic and superstitious simplicity. It is all very severe."

Emile Bernard: Breton Women In The Green Meadow, 1888 - Oil on canvas - St. Germain-en-Laye, private collection.

The diagram shows the way in which the composition is arranged. The foreground is devoted to the womens' head-dresses. Colour is applied in large blocks and the severity of the forms confers a powerful symbolist quality on them.

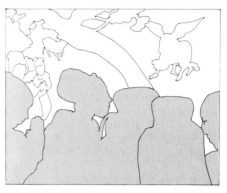

The influence on Gauguin of the Japanese masters (as in the print by Hokusai 1760 - 1849 - The Wrestlers) was part of a widespread fashion. Many artists of the period were fascinated by Japanese art, with its disregard for perspective, flat areas of colour and dramatic cropping. Gauguin seems to have been influenced also by Japanese depictions of wrestlers, which exactly foreshadows his work.

THE YELLOW CHRIST

1889 - Oil on canvas, 92 x 73 cm
Buffalo, Albright-Knox Art Museum

Dramatic Romanesque and ornate Gothic calvaries (crucifixes in shrines) preside over almost every Breton crossroads, village square and thoroughfare. Gauguin could not avoid being impressed by them, and they were the inspiration for a similar work entitled *The Green Christ*.
The Yellow Christ was originally inspired by the polychrome wooden crucifix in the Chapel of Tremalo, a kilometre from Pont-Aven. The flat, unvariegated yellow was intended, he said, to express his feelings about the desolate isolation and medieval feel of Breton life, though possibly the yellowish stain of the actual crucifix itself first suggested the colour to Gauguin. Equally possible is that the idea behind this subject can be traced to a poem *Le Calvaire*, published in *La Revue Indepéndante* in June 1889 by Marie Krysinka, one of the pioneers of Symbolist poetry. In either case, such sources show how very far Gauguin had by this

Gauguin was very attached to this Christ, starkly yellow in its death pallor. This is apparent from his self-portrait, painted the same year - Oil on canvas, 38 x 46 cm - Private collection. The Yellow Christ is behind him, faithfully reproduced in the mirror.

time come from the Impressionists, with their careful sober observation of the natural world around them. There is little that is natural about this painting.
From 1888 to 1891, Gauguin increasingly chose unnaturalistic colours - colours that do not reflect directly the outer world - in a way which might appear arbitrary to the viewer but for the knowledge that it stems directly

from the painter's emotions. Blocks of colour, charged with meaning, form a simple, balanced composition which emphasises the symbolism of his work. The canvas itself plays an important role, its weave and texture often being visible under the fine layers of colour. This technique was increasingly used by Gauguin in his paintings from this time on.

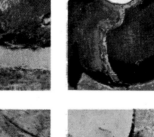

COMPOSITION
The apparent simplicity of the composition conceals a stroke of genius: the cross on which the Yellow Christ is nailed is partially surrounded by a curve formed by the three women in blue, and it is positioned slightly to the left. The effect is to create space on the right, which opens out onto the background of greenish-yellow hills, highlighted by orange-red trees. This space seems to be an invitation to kneel at the feet of the Son of God, whose suffering and humanity are underlined by the unreal, yet intensely dramatic and gripping use of yellow.

PALETTE
The red trees, blue clothes and pink of the head-dress in the foreground stand out against the yellows of the figure of Christ and the background, which is given depth by touches of translucent blue.

THE BEAUTIFUL ANGELE

1889 - Oil on canvas, 92 cm x 73 cm
Paris, Musée d'Orsay

In a letter dated September 1889, addressed to his brother Vincent, Theo Van Gogh described this work: "It is a portrait which is composed on the canvas like those in Japanese prints - a half length figure against a background. It is of a seated Breton woman, her hands clasped in her lap. She is dressed in black, with a lilac apron and white collar. She is framed by a grey surround and the background is a beautiful lilac blue with grey and red flowers. Her expression recalls that of a young cow, yet there is something about her that is so fresh and so open that it becomes almost pleasant." It is hardly surprising that Angèle Satre, who was considered one of the most beautiful women in Pont-Aven, rejected this picture when Gauguin presented it to her! Gauguin had recently visited Degas in Paris, and had admired the older artist's copy of Holbein's portrait of Anne Of Cleves, which was probably the original source for this picture. But this was also the period when Gauguin and others were beginning to question all the principles of modern naturalism. His new style of painting reflected his desire to explore beyond the world of outward appearance and penetrate the secrets of the soul through the manipulation of form and colour. Degas' art, he later said, smelt too much of the model, namely that it was too realistic. As with many of Gauguin's mature works, the arrangement of the elements in *The Beautiful Angèle* conform less to principles of naturalism, and more to his newly formed ideas of symbolism and decorative art.

The Japanese masters of Ukiyo-e (literally, "scenes from the floating world") liked to combine different formats in their compositions by introducing circular forms within the overall rectangle of their painting. They called this the "competition of picture with a picture". There were instruction manuals describing this form of painting, which was frequently used on lacquered boxes. Gauguin, who lived in an age obsessed by Japanese art, also employed this technique, juxtaposing the realism of the portrait, enclosed within an arc of a circle, with the mystery of a decorative border of flowers animated by the presence of an idol. The two illustrations above demonstrate the similarity of outline and pose between the woman and the idol.

Utagawa Kuniyoshi: The Beautiful Tokiwa - Gozen, 1843 - Coloured woodcut, 37 x 24 cm - Private collection.

TA MATETE
(THE MARKET)

1892 - Oil on canvas, 78 x 92 cm
Basle, Oeffentliche Kunstsammlung

TA MATETE

Gauguin abandoned Paris and civilisation in his quest for a simplicity, an almost religious truth and innocence among the peoples of the South Sea Islands but he took with him both his classical European background and also the fruits of his more recent researches into non-European and primitive art. Significantly, he was clearly influenced by Egyptian art when he painted *Ta Matete*.

This simple, precise composition in which the figures have been arranged in a rhythmic succession of colours illustrates Gauguin's words: "The truth ... is that the most sophisticated primitive art of all is that of Egypt." Egyptian (like Byzantine) art appealed to the Symbolists, with whom he was then on such close terms, because of its rejection of naturalism, its hieratic poses and all its mysterious connotations. But as always it is his painting which triumphs over any bookish ideas or historical theories.

Gauguin uses colour as always with great style. The red stands out against the foreground. The yellow, orange-red, grey and olive green colours of the dresses of the seated women stand out in contrast with the warm browns of their faces and hands. The dark colours, the blues and browns of the figures in the background are set off by the pale pink-grey of the ground. It is a magnificent painting, a fine demonstration of his new style.

The women sitting next to each other in their traditional pose recall clearly those in a fresco which decorated an Egyptian tomb at Thebes of the XVIIIth dynasty (British Museum, London). This composition is also very reminiscent of an Egyptian bas-relief preserved at the Louvre (above) in which the women are represented in an identical position, but in a mirror image.

"I shall always believe in the art which is still to be created in the Tropics... I believe that it will be marvellous. But personally, I am too old... Will Gauguin do it?"

Van Gogh to his brother Theo

"Daudet talks enthusiastically about Gauguin who wants to go to Tahiti to be alone but who never actually leaves, so that even his very best friends end up saying to him: 'You must go, dear friend, you must go."

Jules Renard

Cover of Noa-Noa, a book written by Gauguin about his impressions of Tahiti

PALETTE

This is different in each of his paintings. However, there are some fundamental colours which make up the basis of his palette: the white of zinc white, the yellow of cadmium or Naples yellow, yellow ochre, vermilion red and lacquer red, violet, Prussian blue and ultramarine blue, cobalt green and emerald green. He often painted on a fabric similar to jute, sometimes without coating it with a ground. This enabled him to make use of the material's opacity and absorbent quality. It was also cheaper - an important point.

Gauguin generally painted with a brush. He only occasionally worked with a knife, adding wax to the pigment of the paint to make it thicker and more opaque. His basic colours were ground by hand, making them granular, unlike the smooth paste of pigments which were produced by machine.

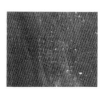

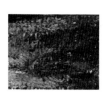

HIS TECHNIQUE

Having first prepared the canvas with a coat of white, he transferred his drawing with the outlines of the figures and the other elements of the painting. He built up the picture with flat tints, filling in the outlines lightly marked in blue so as to make the coloured silhouettes stand out, thus emphasizing the succession of tones. He thinned the paint on some of the figures so that the grain of the canvas showed up, creating a luminous, transparent effect. He applied a further coat to the dry paint of other figures, so as to apply the flat tints more easily. For the background and the figures in the middle ground he allowed the canvas to show through the first transparent coat. The colours of the clothes, yellow, orange, grey, green and dark green, stand out against the light grey background.

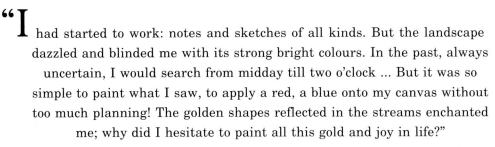

"**I** had started to work: notes and sketches of all kinds. But the landscape dazzled and blinded me with its strong bright colours. In the past, always uncertain, I would search from midday till two o'clock ... But it was so simple to paint what I saw, to apply a red, a blue onto my canvas without too much planning! The golden shapes reflected in the streams enchanted me; why did I hesitate to paint all this gold and joy in life?"

From Noa Noa by Gauguin

SIESTA

1891-92 - Oil on canvas, 87 x 116 cm
Walter H. Annenberg

In the tropics, the siesta was a well-nigh universal custom, to escape the worst heat of the day. But here none of the characters are actually asleep; they are acting as models, consciously or not, for the white man with his brush, as if enacting their roles. Almost all Gauguin's paintings of the Tahitian people were of women, and he delighted in their beauty and in their legendary readily-available charms. He was also not averse to feeding the desires of his potential buyers who were, of course, almost all men. The diagonal of the composition is interrupted by the coloured shapes of the other characters: the pink of the woman on the left, the bright red of the young girl lying down, the brown of the woman ironing, and the pale pink silhouette against the green background. Such strong, simple colours are the hallmark of his mature style, as is the unnatural yellow of the grass; in the tropics, however, such colours may have seemed closer to nature.

Gauguin wrote in his book *Before And After*: "Always use colours of the same origin ... With patience you will be able to use every shade. Let your paper lighten your colours and make them white, but never leave it totally bare. Who says that light vermilion is flesh-coloured and that linen is shaded with grey? Place a white cloth next to a cabbage or a bunch of flowers and you will see whether the white is tinted with grey. Reject black and the mixture of white and black which is called grey. Nothing is black and nothing is grey. What looks like grey is in fact light hues which an experienced eye can detect."

As always Gauguin has been very attentive to the overall balance of the composition and the importance of the foreground in relation to the other figures. Here the figure of a girl with her back to us cuts the scene diagonally, harmonising with the curved shapes of the other characters.

In 1897 Gauguin painted The Dream - Oil on canvas - 95 x 130 cm, Courtauld Institute Galleries - in which the woman on the left has been borrowed from The Siesta. In the course of a few years the artist has moved from the happiness of a painting expressed in joyful light colours to a darker, heavier approach characterized by the muted colours of the imposingly massive human forms.

WHERE DO WE COME FROM? WHAT ARE WE? WHERE ARE WE GOING TO?

1897 - Oil on canvas, 139 x 374 cm
Boston, Museum of Fine Arts, Tompkins
Collection

This, undoubtedly the greatest work of Gauguin's later career, was in fact intended as a last testament. Racked by illness and utterly disillusioned, he made an unsuccessful suicide attempt (by swallowing huge quantities of arsenic) soon after finishing it. Clearly he wished to leave something tremendous to be remembered by - a masterpiece on a huge scale. Accordingly, he ordered from his correspondent de Monfreid in Paris vast quantities of paint and canvas. He worked frantically day and night to finish it in one month.

The portentous title of the painting clearly reflects his state of mind at the time, but was in fact added later, when he had recovered from the stomach cramps following his self-poisoning. The mysterious titles he gave most of his Pacific paintings normally failed to impress either his supporters or his detractors at home; the former thought them unnecessary adornments for such superb pictures, the latter agreed with Pissarro, his earlier mentor, who accused Gauguin of "plundering the themes of Oceanic art like an artistic colonialist."

Several of the figures originate in his earlier works; the entire composition recalls a painting by the Symbolist Puvis de Chavannes, exhibited in 1890 - yet another example of how Gauguin never escaped the influence of western art in his Pacific idyll. The figures, glowing resplendently solid in their golden flesh, are arranged as in a frieze, with very little obvious connection between them. Gauguin later explained that the old woman on the left referred to Where Are We

Drawing of Where Do We Come From? What Are We? Where Are We Going To? in a letter which Gauguin wrote to his friend Daniel de Monfreid in 1898.

In Self-Portrait Of The Artist With A Palette, painted in 1888 and dedicated to Van Gogh, Gauguin seems to have drawn his eyes asking the same questions as the painting - what is the meaning of life, work and death?

Nave Nave Mahama, 1896 - Oil on canvas, 95 x 130 cm - Lyon, Musée des Beaux-Arts. This is another typically paradisiacal picture Gauguin painted on his return to Tahiti from Paris.

Going? while on the right the newborn baby posed the question Where Do we come from? The two "sinister figures in garments of sombre colour" behind the tree in the centre-right apparently referred to the tree of good and evil in the Garden of Eden - that paradise Gauguin had hoped but failed to find intact in the Pacific. In March 1899 he wrote to the hostile art critic André Fontainas: "Talking about that canvas again: the idol is not there as a literary explanation, but as a statue; maybe less of a statue than an animal figure; less animal also, being part of my dream, of my hut surrounded by the whole of nature. It rules our primitive soul, an imaginary consolation for our suffering caused."

The old woman on the left, crouching and holding her head in her hands, is reminiscent of characters in previous paintings, such as the pastel-and-watercolour shown on the left, entitled Breton Eve. The figure of the child eating fruit next to a goat has been taken from Nave Nave Mahama.

The sketch clearly shows the essentially classical structure of the composition which is based on the central figure. Here this figure is slightly off-centre, to the right of the axis. There is a triangular arrangement in each of the two halves of the rectangle making up the canvas. The left triangle almost completely encloses the idol, while the one on the right contains a group of figures.

The central figure with raised arms was inspired by Rembrandt's study of a nude, in the Musée du Louvre, of which Gauguin had made a sketch.

Tahitian Pastorale, 1898 - Oil on canvas, 54 x 169 cm - London, Tate Gallery. In this painting Gauguin's colours depart still further from reality. Its composition recalls Botticelli's Spring; Gauguin had pinned a reproduction of Spring to his hut wall.

THE WHITE HORSE

1898 - Oil on canvas, 140 x 91 cm
Paris, Musée d'Orsay

The style of Gauguin's last years made use of large areas of flat tints, bright, luminous colours, a balanced, rigorously worked-out composition, and a symbolic, avowedly mystical approach. This is perfectly illustrated in *The White Horse*, perhaps derived from a relief from the west frieze of the Parthenon in Athens. A closer and perhaps more important source was Degas.

In the foreground is a white horse, whose legs disappear into the cobalt blue of the pond illuminated by orange-coloured reflections. The red horse in the middle ground stands out against the green of the meadow and the blue of the shimmering water. Everything in this painting shows Gauguin's style in its late maturity. First, the harmony of the composition whose curves resemble those of a ballet (indeed Gauguin often compared painting to music in his writings). This is most beautifully illustrated in the curves of the white horse's neck and back which is perfectly matched by the sinuous outlines of the blue branches dividing the canvas diagonally. The choice and association of colours are totally detached from reality, creating a fantastic, self-sufficient landscape which is a forerunner of Fauvism, the school of artists in Paris which, emerging in 1905, was vastly influenced by Gauguin and whose name means significantly "wild beasts".

Gauguin wanted his composition to convey a fantastic world filled with emotion. This is why he chose unreal colours: the red horse, the inky river and trees, the tender green of the meadow, and the shimmering gold of the path.

"**H**ere, near my hut, in complete silence, I dream of violent harmonies in the natural fragrances which intoxicate me. I sense exalted delights of some unknown sacred horror from an immeasurably distant past. Also in the past, the perfume of joy which I am breathing at this moment. Animal figures with the rigidity of a statue: I sense something ancient, majestic and religious in the rhythm of their movements, in their extraordinary immobility. In the eyes which dream, is the troubled surface of an unfathomable enigma. And then it is night - everything is at rest. My eyes close to see a dream in the infinity of space which escapes from me without understanding, and I am aware of the sad passing of my hopes."

from Noa-Noa

COMPOSITION
The branches of the trees, the silhouette of the horse and the river bank form a succession of curving lines. These give a very enclosed, hot and dense jungle impression, accentuated by the sinister beauty of the flower in the right foreground.

TAHITIAN GIRLS WITH FLOWERS

1899 - Oil on canvas, 94 x 72.2 cm
New York, Metropolitan Museum of Art,
Gift of W. C. Osborne.

After Gauguin's return from Paris in 1895, when he realised that his exile in the Pacific was now to be permanent and irrevocable, he painted many more, sometimes striking, pictures of Tahitian society, but few are as beautiful and as forceful as this. Even its subjects - mango-blossoms, the archetypal flowers of the Tropics, and half-naked, beautiful young girls - represent the perfect dream of the South Sea islands where all was innocent and beautiful. In fact, his last years were not at all idyllic, troubled as they were with recurrent illnesses, increasing difficulties with the colonial authorities and financial problems. This painting therefore, should be seen both as wish-fulfilment and as a valediction, for in his very last years he completed relatively few paintings.

Gauguin was fascinated by the classic beauty, bearing and behaviour of Tahitian women, in whom he seems to have found magical echoes of ancient Greek beauty. He tried to convey this magic in his portraits by exaggerating a pose to make it more expressive. It is difficult to remain indifferent when looking at the slightly-bowed head of the young girl holding the basket of flowers. Her pensive eyes and the sweet unspoken (but unmistakable) invitation exert a magical effect on the viewer. The two young girls are not just offering a basket of flowers; these totally innocent female nudes represent a primordial vitality, filled with a happiness and purity which captured the artist's heart. He has endowed them with a monumental solidity that looks back to Greek art.

Head Of A Young Tahitian Girl - *1891-1901 - Chicago, The Art Institute, Gift of David Adler and his friends.*
These two drawings are reminiscent of the attitude of the two girls in the painting.

"I was working in great haste - knowing that these feelings would not last forever - in haste and with passion. I have put into this portrait what my heart allowed my eyes to see, and what the eyes alone could not see."

from Noa-Noa

RIDERS ON THE BEACH

1902 - Oil on canvas, 66 x 76 cm
Essen, Folkwang Museum

Gauguin moved finally to Hivaoa (Dominica) in the Marquesas Islands. Although even in this final settling place he did not find tranquility at least his paintings show a little of his elusive happiness. His happiness exploded in his art in the sumptuous lyricism of his colours which again glowed with their fantastic sparkle and dazzling brightness.

As always, there are references to western art - most notably, to Degas, the master of such equestrian scenes, whose works Gauguin had so often and so frequently studied. There is also of course a symbolic meaning in the figures of the young horsemen who seem to be riding towards freedom and happiness on the pink sand of the beach. Gauguin had always enjoyed physical pursuits such as horse-riding. The central perspective of the painting, leading to the sea and to the distant island, dominates the picture. The three riders seen from behind, on their dark horses, are balanced by the two figures on the left riding white horses and wearing bright hooded shirts.

The dominant colours are the pink of the beach, which almost fills the whole of the bottom half of the canvas, and the blue band of the sea. There is a harmony between these colours and the browns of the riders with their blue and green trousers and the dull whites of the two horses. The pink aura of a distant island on the horizon and the sinuous lines of the tree trunks on the right add mysterious and sym-

Although Gauguin loved painting the soft, sensual figures of the women of Tahiti, he also enjoyed painting half-clothed young riders mounted on their fiery horses. In this painting of 1901 called The Flight - Oil on canvas, 73 x 92 cm - Moscow, Pushkin Museum - the silhouettes of the riders, a light patch and a dark one, stand out against the cool colours of the forest.

The orange and the yellow of the riders' clothes and the blue of the sea contrast and sometimes clash dramatically with the background shades.

bolic elements to the picture. Gauguin has given the scene an atmosphere of timelessness and detachment, conveying a kind of serene savagery by purely formal means. It was this savagery which was to appeal so much to Fauvists like Matisse soon afterwards in France, when they saw his art.

THE QUEST FOR THE PRIMITIVE

Gauguin was well on the way to becoming a wealthy stockbroker when he discovered a passion for painting. This was around 1874, a significant date as it was the year of the First Impressionist Exhibition, which caused a stir. Gauguin came to side with these revolutionaries who were renewing painters' ways of seeing - and transforming their ways of painting. This they achieved by means of direct contact with nature and the observation of the effects of light and atmosphere which change the actual substance of forms and exalt the strength of colour.

In fact, Gauguin never completely subscribed to the theories of Impressionism and the joyful explosion of colour and light which characterised the movement. He stuck to more traditional composition, and a solidity of matter showing a different view of reality.

Less than ten years after the First Impressionist Exhibition, the movement was already in crisis. This was not just an isolated crisis in a group of painters, but a questioning of the principles of modern naturalism which affected all fields of thought and art. A need to go beyond the world of appearances to penetrate the secrets of the human soul began to be felt. External reality, for true Impressionists the only subject worth considering, was being challenged by the world of inner ideas and inspiration - in short, Symbolism.

Symbolism was a reaction not just against the Impressionists but against a whole school of realism that had dominated French culture for decades. In painting, the greatest exponents of realism were Gustave Courbet and Theodore Rousseau, both influential landscape painters, while in literature the grimly realistic novels of

GAUGUIN AND HIS TIMES

	HIS LIFE AND WORKS	HISTORY	ART AND CULTURE
1848	Born in Paris	Fall of the July Monarchy in France "Year of Revolutions" throughout Europe Third Chartist Petition in London	Thomas Macaulay: *History of England* Pre-Raphaelite brotherhood of painters formed by Holman Hunt, John Millais and Dante Gabriel Rossetti
1865	Joins the navy, where he remains for six years	End of the American Civil War Assassination of President Lincoln Lord Russell becomes Prime Minister on the death of Lord Palmerston	Lewis Carroll: *Alice in Wonderland* Richard Wagner: *Tristan And Isolde* Birth of the poet W. B. Yeats
1871	Starts to work as a stockbroker but is already interested in painting	Commune of Paris suppressed German Empire proclaimed with William I as emperor Trade Unions Act in Britain allows unions to own property	Charles Darwin: *The Descent Of Man* Arthur Rimbaud: *Le Bâteau Ivre* Giuseppe Verdi: *Aida*
1873	Marries the Danish Mette Sophie Gad	Proclamation of republic in Spain Mac Mahon becomes President of France	Tolstoy starts *Anna Karenina* J.F. Millet: *Spring*
1876	*Landscape At Viroflay* exhibited in the Salon	Serbia and Montenegro revolt v Turkey Education Act establishes compulsory primary education in Britain	Mark Twain: *The Adventures of Tom Sawyer.* Renoir: *Ball At The Moulin Rouge*
1880	First exhibition with the Impressionists	Tahiti becomes a French colony	Dostoyevsky: *The Brothers Karamazov* Norman Shaw starts building Bedford Park
1881	Works with Cézanne. Second exhibition with the Impressionists	Czar Alexander II assassinated Second Irish Land Act gives Irish tenants security of tenure	Birth of Picasso
1883	Abandons his family and job to devote himself to painting.	Brititish protectorate established in Egypt; French protectorate established in Vietnam	Friedrich Nietzsche starts *Thus Spoke Zarathustra* Robert Louis Stevenson: *Treasure Island*
1886	Goes to Pont-Aven where he meets Emile Bernard and to Paris, where he meets the Van Gogh brothers. Exhibits with the Impressionists	Discovery of gold on The Rand Gladstone's Irish Home Rule Bill rejected by House of Lords	Saint-Saëns: *Carnival of The Animals* *Le Figaro* publishes Symbolist manifesto

Emile Zola, depicted a drab industrial world that poets and painters felt a frantic need to escape. Symbolism degenerated into a stifling hot-house of morbid and often mediocre art, epitomised by the luxurious pictures of Gustave Moreau, in which bejewelled princes suffer unlikely fates in ornate palaces.

Such decadence and artifice might seem far removed from Gauguin's burning thirst for the primitive, which he found in simple Brittany and Tahiti. But Gauguin never believed in too close an imitation of nature; his style moved further from naturalism than either Van Gogh or Cézanne, both of whom Gauguin revered.

Above all, he wished to free colour from the tyranny of pure representation. For this reason, the influence of primitive or non-European art - from Peru, Java, the Pacific and Japan - was vital to the development of his art. And his wish to escape from everyday tedium united him with the dreams of the Symbolists. Paradoxically, Gauguin remained a great admirer of the pure classical tradition in French and Italian art - Raphael, Ingres, Degas - whose markedly sculptural qualities are evident in his art. Gauguin also sculpted and made wood cuts.

Brittany was the first "primitive" place to inspire Gauguin. On his three visits to the artists' colony of Pont-Aven there in the late 1880s, he met several artists, most notably the younger but forceful Emile Bernard. Bernard was something of a mystic, who found in the unreformed and wildly superstitious rustic Catholicism of Breton villagers the inspiration he needed to produce paintings in a novel style called cloisonnism. This was typified by dark outlines enclosing areas of bright, flat colour similar

1887	Goes to Panama and Martinique. Begins to differ from Impressionism	Italians overwhelmingly defeated by the Ethiopians at Dogali	Georges Seurat: *Circus Parade* Van Gogh starts his *Sunflowers*
1888	Develops Synthetism at Pont-Aven with Bernard. Paints *The Vision After The Sermon*. Joins Van Gogh at Arles; in December he returns to Paris	William II becomes Emperor of Germany. Cecil Rhodes acquires the future Rhodesia (Zimbabwe)	Birth of T.S. Eliot August Strindberg: *Miss Julie*
1889	Exhibition at Café Volpini a financial failure but a critical success. *The Yellow Christ*; Symbolist influence	World Fair at Paris Second Socialist International set up British South Africa Company formed to promote imperial expansion	Death of Robert Browning Jerome K. Jerome: *Three Men In A Boat* W.B. Yeats: *Crossways*
1891	First visit to Tahiti. Paints *On The Beach*	Creation of German East Africa (now Tanzania)	Herman Melville: *Billy Budd* Toulouse-Lautrec: *Dance At The Moulin Rouge* Thomas Hardy: *Tess Of The D'Urbevilles*
1893	Returns to Paris. Fails to impress buyers or critics despite winning the admiration of Bonnard and Degas	Gladstone introduces Second Home Rule bill for Ireland; rejected by the House of Lords	Puccini: *Manon Lescaut* W.B. Yeats: *The Rose*
1895	Leaves Paris finally for Tahiti	Start of the Dreyfus Affair in France Rontgen discovers X-rays Trial and imprisonment of Oscar Wilde	Rudyard Kipling: *The Jungle Book (part 2)* Sigmund Freud: *Studies In Hysteria*
1897	Paints his masterpiece *Where Do We Come From? What Are We? Where Are Going To?* in December	Queen Victoria's Diamond Jubilee First legal compensation for industrial injuries	Richard Strauss: *Don Quixote* Henri Rousseau : *The Sleeping Gypsy*
1898	Attempts suicide on a mountain by swallowing arsenic; recovers	Death of Bismarck, German Chancellor Battle of Omdurman; Kitchener defeats the Mahdi in the Sudan Pierre and Marie Curie discover radium	H. G. Wells: *War Of The Worlds* Oscar Wilde: *The Ballad Of Reading Gaol* Death of Aubrey Beardsley
1901	Escapes colonial authority by fleeing to the Marquesas Islands	Assassination of President MacKinley in USA; succeeded by Theodore Roosevelt Death of Queen Victoria	Anton Chekhov: *The Three Sisters* Thomas Mann: *Buddenbroks* Rudyard Kipling: *Kim*
1903	In March he is condemned to three months' imprisonment. Riddled with disease, he dies 18 May	The Wright Brothers' first plane flight Split between Russian Bolsheviks (led by Lenin) and the Mensheviks	Henry James: *The Ambassadors* Bernard Shaw: *Man And Superman* Birth of Evelyn Waugh

to stained glass or cloisonné enamels (cloison means partition in French). Bernard's later claims to have alone invented cloisonnism were dismissed by Gauguin, but the paintings he did at this time (*The Vision After The Sermon,* page 8 or *The Yellow Christ,* page 10) mark the dramatic arrival of his own mature style.

Those pictures of between 1888 and 1891 used arbitrary, unnatural colour (bright reds or yellows for the fields, for example), for emotional rather than realistic effect, applied in wide, simple strokes. Space lacks real depth in these spiritual visions, with their symbolic and literary evocations, often mystical and religious in tone. Bernard's mysticism undoubtedly influenced Gauguin's choice of themes and style, but the young theorist never attained the same levels of symbolic art as his older friend.

A CLASSICAL PRIMITIVE

The years around 1890 were Gauguin's time of fame: many painters followed him to Brittany, to what became known as the "School of Pont-Aven". Others in Paris considered him to be the prophet of a new language and style of painting, while poets were interested in his art. O. Mirbeau, a critic, described this art as simultaneously "complicated and primitive, clear and obscure, barbaric and refined". Gauguin, with his massive rough-hewn silhouette, became an important figure in Symbolist circles. He was a regular visitor to their meeting places, particularly the Café Voltaire. In 1891, the year of the triumph of Symbolism, his canvases sold successfully at the auction. Yet Gauguin had finally decided to leave Paris for the tropics.

His first experiment on the Island of Tahiti lasted from 1891 to 1893. Despite ecstatic letters to the contrary, he found the island had already been half-corrupted by civilisation - particularly missionaries, who had persuaded many Tahitian women to wear western clothes, to the painter's disgust. On his canvases, however, he celebrated the joy of a simple and pure life in the blinding light of the sky or the warm shadow of the luxuriant vegetation.

He celebrated the sensuality of bodies as exuberant and as fresh as flowers, or the mystery of the spirits that watched over the tribe. His colour harmonies, which attempted to give symbolic expression to a spiritual dimension, were richly sumptuous and provided the form for a total Synthetism. These canvases, such as *Ta Matete* (page 14) which were given a cool reception at the famous galleries of the dealer Durand-Ruel in Paris, were not simply "exotic"; they revealed the influences of all primitive arts.

However, there was a common thread between the naive rough-carved crucifixes in Brittany, and the ritual, symbolic images of these primitive Pacific peoples, who carved basic, powerful, non-naturalistic forms personifying the forces of nature with deep religious feeling. Gauguin wanted to recreate their innermost motives, while knowing that his desires and fears were those of a modern man, with an aesthetic heritage and emotional reactions totally different from those of a Pacific islander. For he could never forget the influence of Degas, whose works he had once assiduously copied, and through Degas the whole of western classicism, with its emphasis on the human form.

It was this approach, combining the primitive with the classical, which led Gauguin to incorporate symbols, laden with spiritual, often mystical meanings, into his depictions of the external world, so that he combined nature and fantasy, truth and imagination. The painted image was a new objective reality, created poetically by Gauguin, not a faithful rendering of the outer world. He wrote: "Primitive art comes from the spirit and makes use of nature. So-called refined art proceeds from sensuality and serves nature. Nature is the servant of the former and the mistress of the latter."

Such beliefs did not always help his sales back home, however. Partly driven by financial worries, he returned to Paris in 1893. His reunion with Parisian circles was a disappointment to him. Despite great social success, he felt out of place in Paris and even in Pont-Aven, which he revisited. In February 1895, he set out for Tahiti once again, resolved never to return.

He now painted what many consider his masterpiece *Where Do We Come From? What Are We? Where Are We Going To?* (page 20) - a piece as monumental in its forms and vivid in its colours as it is mysterious in its title. After finishing this masterpiece successfully, he unsuccessfully attempted suicide, depressed among other things by news of his favourite daughter Aline's death. Further vivid canvases followed his recovery, depicting a passionately sensual paradise which owed as much to his dreams as to his experiences, such as *Tahitian Girls With Flowers* (page 26). Western classicism and primitive sculptures had here merged together in a new reality created by Paul Gauguin.